Love, Loss, and Inspiration

Karen Benckenstein

BookLeaf Publishing

India | USA | UK

Presentation by *BookLeaf Publishing*

Web: www.bookleafpub.com

E-mail: info@bookleafpub.com

ISBN: 9789360947781

First edition 2024

To my mother and son, who made this possible.

Boundless

To live without a template
In a way that is deliberate
And full of joy.
To define choice
By the true desires
Of your heart.
Not by how hard
Not by what
Might stop you.
But what you need to do
To release control
And surrender
To love.

Stranger

I'm not from here.
I'm a stranger renting this body, a tenant of this
mind.
I'll be gone before you know it,
But what will I leave behind?
With any luck, some magic.
Some love and smiles, to boot.
And the message that we don't belong here,
But I helped to find some truth.

About Writing

I write because I was put here to write.
I write because I'm told I must.
I write because I can.
When talents and passions were handed out
Writing seems to have been mine.
And yet, it feels like pulling my fingernails out
with pliers
Sometimes.
I write about writing
Because it is the lowest hanging fruit.
Write what you know,
They say.
Writing is always on my mind.
Whether it's a story idea,
A poem,
An analogy for life,
An idea for an article,
Or just itching to write.
I don't know that I know writing,
But it is certainly what fills my mind.
It is how I process thoughts
And ideas.
When people wax philosophical about
Meaning
Purpose

Goals.
I think of writing.
And I actually feel guilt for not doing it more.

I Love Me

I love you.
I love you.
I love you.
When will I believe it?
I love you.
You with the eyes that saw my father before he
left.
I love you.
You with the hand that held my sister's before
she died.
I love you.
You with the breasts that fed my son,
The body that wasn't enough for his father.
I love you.
You with the mouth that struggles to speak your
own truth.
I love you.
Maybe I do.
I love you.
I will treat you better.
I love you.
I will be kind to you.
I will honor you.
I really do love you.

Women Friends

Women friends:
The joy they give,
The lives they live…
It's vital.
This power gained from time
With friends.
The memories, shared or not.
The laughter, sweet and hot.
The music, loud and poignant.
The food, plentiful and abundant.
It's necessary.
It's beautiful.
The young one venture by,
Not knowing how much
They will need this.
And we cling tight,
Not knowing how long
We will have this.
Girl time.
Christmas parties.
Drunk dancing.
This is life lived full.

Match

Burning brightly
Passion
You bock us
And call us
Old fashioned
Grandmothers burned
For speaking
Out of turn.
You can't silence
Us so easily.
Successful
Beautiful
Desirable
Out of control
It is all the things
We want to be
And all the things
We don't want
To be told
Strong women-
May she be one
Flame to tip-
I pass it on.
Mountains burning
A nation churning

They say
we can't choose
We say,
"Watch us."
We start with choosing to burn.
We start with taking our turn.

Ladies First

Ladies first.
Thank you so much.

What do we exchange
For this small privilege?
Watch your back
Watch your weight
Watch your words
Don't deny him a touch

Ladies first
You beat us to the punch.

Through all the years
and the hardship
First to bleed
First to blame
First to smile
He can't help his lust

Thank you the same
But i will go last

If you can just wait
Wait to judge me

Wait to hurt me
Wait to know me
Before deciding what's best

I think it could be
Ladies last

We will wait our turn
To be in charge
To have our rights
To be equal
We won't interrupt

But once we are there
We will indeed be

Ladies first
First to lead
First to teach
First to win
We won't give up

Hell

I know how
They greet you in hell
Limp handshakes
And insincere hugs
Anything worth doing
Is worth doing well

Depression

12

Sadness and depression
The paper's edge
Screw the knife
The paper is thinner
And you don't know
Which side you're on

Disordered Eating

Cookies, warm and moist,
smell of shame and guilt.
Pot roast, hot and dry,
Reminds me of a quilt-
Warm, familiar, old.

Food holds me down
Like a straitjacket
Like a rope that is bound
To suffocate me.

But it is medicine.
It is nourishing.
Not a deadly sin.
Not a poison.

Show me how to eat
Without hiding.
Show me how to grow
Without fighting
This urge everyday.
Show me how to shrink
Without purging.
Show me how to learn
Without constant urging.

New Year Resolutions

The light doesn't last as long now.
The time inside, by the fire, with loved ones
Increases.
The days of lazy hammocks,
Swimming, laying in the sun,
Sleeping till noon
Are past.
We pause,
We take a breath
And count our blessings.
We resolve to do better
In the days
Of long sun.
But how quickly we will forget
When the days are long again.

My Sister Died in Autumn

I sit on my porch and write.
I sit on my porch and cry.
I sit on my porch and drink
red wine.
I remember all our beautiful memories.

The temperature gets colder.
The wine turns to water.
The seasons change
too quickly
just as she passed much too soon.

Sister

Did you hear that?
That was the sound
Of my last thread snapping
Hope somebody
Can catch me.
Can't get it out of my head:
My sister is dead.
She was my biggest fan,
My right hand man,
She held my hand.
Through thick and thin,
Lose and win,
Blessing and sin.
She knew
where the bodies were buried,
My maid of honor
When I married.
And a shoulder to cry on
When I divorced.
Now I'm forced
To accept
She is the one in the ground.
It hurts too much
The wound still too
Tender to touch.

Not sure how to deal
Not sure I'll ever heal.

Angel Wings

18

So loved,
If only for a moment.
No one will ever
Know you as I did.
You heard
My heartbeat
From the inside.
You never had one.
This mark
You've left on my heart.
This mark
I made on my body.

My Motherhood

I always wanted to be a mom.
I dreamed of tiny hands and feet.
I waited so very long
With no baby of my own.
Two children died to heaven
The pain still in my bones.
My son finally came to me
Blood of my blood.
But I'm now mother of six-
Of my body and my love.
Two ended before they began,
One mine from toddler on,
One in the way of ancestors,
And two belonging first to my man.
I always wanted to be a mother,
But never imagined how.
I'm so grateful for my children
And that I'm a mother now.

Sarge

He ran behind a stranger
Accepting love where he could find it.
She offered him so water,
And the stranger just denied him.

As a puppy he chewed and chewed.
But as an adult, he is more chill
We share a bed, affection, and food.

I'm so grateful for this pup.
He's loyal always
And so full of love.

Wishing Well

I wish, I wish upon this star
What am I wishing for?
I wish, I wish in this wishing well
What I wish for, I will not tell.

I made a wish
And it came true
Came true
When I met you.

I made another wish
What would it be?
I wished
For you and me.

Now what is my wish?
My wish is to be
All that I can
All that I want
And wish for me.

Forgotten Love

It was so long ago
That I loved you.
So long ago
That I'm not even sure
It's true.

Did I ever know you?
Did you ever know me?
Did you ever think
This is what we would be?

I wouldn't know you now
If I passed you in a store
I don't know who you are
Or even who you were.

I have forgotten you,
My one time love.
Have you forgotten me?
And what our love
Was made of?

www.ingramcontent.com/pod-product-compliance
Lightning Source LLC
LaVergne TN
LVHW041300200726
843507LV00014B/3074